Author's Note: This was written around August 16, 2018. Midterm struggles are heating up. The House of Representatives, while on vacation at the moment, has plenty of time to smash through some of the below mentioned items. Also, some of these Representatives might not be in office by this time next year. Good luck!

NUMBERING THE 435: HOW MUCH HAS YOUR REPRESENTATIVE DONE FOR YOU?

Volume 1, Edition 1

Introduction:

Taking a somewhat politically biased look at your current Representatives. I chose to start off with one Congresswoman who was on TV the other day, one more for direct comparison, and a few others from her starting year. All were freshman in 2011.

I only look at legislation that they're the primary sponsor of. It's easy to hop on a bandwagon and co-sponsor something; of all the ones below I recall seeing well over a hundred co-sponsored legislations, usually 700+. It's a better measure as to what they've done themselves in my opinion to look at what they've been the sponsor of, at least as far as effectiveness goes. Just voting for something is nothing; any computer from the 1950s onward could take that job as partisan as things are today. Besides, Conservative Review already tallies what their votes go towards. Even if you're a Leftist, Conservative Review is a good guide; just think of the percentages as you would golf scores.

Generally to save time- mine and yours- I don't elaborate on legislation unless it catches my eye. Don't take it to mean that I don't care for their other stuff, sure it's possible that I don't but I also might have just counted it without reading what it was. The main focus of this guide is on quantity of achievements, despite how often I delve into quality.

The 2017-2018 Session information only covers up to 16 August 2018.

Frederica Wilson (D-FL)

Her record does not jibe with the attention she receives. Lately she is best known for declaring that she wanted to cuss out President Trump when he had an awkward call to a gold star mother, and for saying on CNN that it's wrong to call a woman of color a name like "whacky", even if said woman goes around wearing a cowboy hat despite being a Congresswoman from Florida, a state not known for its cowboy heritage.

She's been the primary sponsor for 82 pieces of legislation. She managed to get two laws passed. One was the glorious, life-changing, poverty-ending, anti-racism law which… named a Federal building in Florida. Inspirational. Another much touted law that surely would end inequality… renamed a post office building. Two of her resolutions passed. Two of her amendments passed as well. Probability makes it peculiar that she'd pass 2 laws, 2 resolutions, and 2 amendments, in her first 6 years *(2+2+2 = 6)*. I suppose it's a safe opinion to have that she's been much more effective playing a Congresswoman on TV, because her TV persona contrasts greatly with her run-of-the-mill legislative record.

Of the 12 bills she sponsored in 2017-2018 none have yet made it past being introduced. 2 of them were Assault Weapons bans; the only one to receive a co-sponsor was introduced just after the Parkland shootings. *(I have to wonder about these bans: since a lot of the companies featured on them make weapons for the military, how would the sudden cut in funding affect their ability to keep rifles up-to-date and meet military demand since so much of their business relies on civilian sales?)*. She had 17 bills 2015-2016, one of which became a law but the rest never made it past being introduced. For the 2013-2014 session she was down to 11 bills, one of which also became a law. In her first term, 2011-2012, she sponsored 11 bills that nothing happened with.

Congresswoman Wilson has introduced 4 concurrent resolutions from 2017-2018. Two of them relate to Haiti, relating to how *(despite the Clinton Foundation's much lauded help)* the country still has not recovered from the 2010 earthquake.

There are 2 resolutions to her name for 2017-2018. One of them is for "Honoring the life of Trayvon Martin, urging the repeal of Stand Your Ground laws". Now, George Zimmerman was acquitted because the jury believed his side of the story *(and the pictures taken right after the incident showing his blood-and-wound covered head)* that Trayvon Martin had been the aggressor and was trying to kill Zimmerman, so basically Wilson believes she knows better than a jury that saw all of the evidence, believes Trayvon was a saint.*Neither resolution passed, by the way. She had 6 resolutions 2015-2016. None of them made it past being introduced, and the Trayvon Martin one was there too. Just as in the 2017-2018 session, there were 0 sponsors this time around. She was much more prolific from 2013-2014 with her resolutions: 12 were introduced, 2 actually passed. Again, nothing came of Trayvon's sainthood and denying people the right to defend themselves, but her two identical measures condemning Boko Haram, introduced a month apart, were agreed to. Her first 3 resolutions, in the 2011-2012 session, went nowhere.

Rep. Wilson saw some success with Amendments in the 2015-2016 session. Of the three she proposed, one was accepted, related to school district transparency regarding the tests they'd give. She had a 100% success rate with amendments from 2013-2014, since she only introduced one. What passed was an amendment calling for transparency with research data on charter schools, data such as class size, academic achievement, and quality of education. Stuff you'd want to know if deciding on which school to send your kids to.

This isn't to say that all of her legislation was such partisan hackery that not even her own party cared about them *(I personally wondered why some items stalled since they looked pretty bipartisan, and would've been totally onboard with her H. R. 5719, if I were certain folks guilty of some possible non-violent crimes like blackmail or fraud would be excluded. Her Drive To Stay Alive bill was also surprising in that it didn't go anywhere.)*. It just means she hasn't been successful on the follow-through.

Given the big deal she made about him before the facts were in, she can hardly be blamed for not wanting to back down. But she does want everyone else to back down- she wants America to have no Stand Your Ground laws, just like the UK. So let's see what that means- in the UK, police on multiple occasions have told citizens they are not allowed to defend themselves from violent criminals; according to the police themselves, citizens are at best allowed rape whistles and a bottle of dye to spray a criminal with in case police are inclined to search for the criminal later, as long as neither implement is used in a way that might hurt a criminal; if either implement harms a criminal then the person using it will be charged. It's illegal to even wave a kitchen knife at potential intruders if you're a woman home alone with your daughter while three men stare into your house.

Daniel Webster (R-FL)

Let's take a look at another Congressman from Florida who started in 2011, and is still in office. He was only the primary sponsor of 37 pieces of legislation. None of his 12 bills became law, though they were for more than renaming buildings. One did pass the House. All 6 of his amendments passed. All 19 of his resolutions passed. So while he's done quantitatively less than Frederica Wilson, he's still passed more resolutions and amendments than she did. Quality is debatable- while his weren't particularly noteworthy, Wilson should've known that repealing Stand Your Ground laws was such a grandstand that it would most certainly have gone nowhere. Webster hasn't been much of a TV presence though. The most press coverage he received was when he ran for House Speaker in 2015. Aside from something his office did during his 2011 campaign, there isn't much controversy at all around him. A nice quiet fellow doing his job, sort of *(he kind of disappeared 2015-2016, but that could be attributed to his two runs for House Speaker and his district being redrawn such that it had more Democrat voters, which caused him to switch districts)*, that you'd never even know existed unless you read this or lived in his district.

Off to an ok start with his bills. Only 4 in 2017-2018, but one had passed the House, his Small Business Cybersecurity Act. Apparently 2015-2016 he was on vacation because all he did was introduce 3 bills that went nowhere. That was a match for 2013-2014, which also saw 3 bills going nowhere, but he had some other items going too that session. 2011-2012 saw only two bills, but none of them passed. One of them looked like something that should've been a bipartisan winner- it would've encouraged companies to hire people that have been receiving federal or state unemployment compensation by giving them a tax credit.

His 2017-2018 Amendment Record is at 100%- he had 2, both passed. Still at 100% for 2013-2014. In a repeat performance of offering two amendments that passed. One of them was for preventing "federal agencies from implementing significant policy changes without appropriate congressional review", basically stopping the Executive Branch from making-up major policy changes that might have the impact of new laws without Congressional oversight, since laws are supposed to be coming from Congress anyway and bypassing Congress by stretching the authority of your branch of government beyond what it credibly could be claimed to be isn't really in keeping with the spirit of the Constitution. His 2011-2012 amendment record again is 100%- 2 sponsored, 2 passed.

2013-2014 saw him sponsor 5 resolutions, and they all were agreed to. Each resolution was designed to allow a bill to be considered. 2011-2012 saw him introduce 14 resolutions, ALL of which were agreed to. They all related to other bills though, allowing them to be considered or in one case asking the Senate to send one back. Honestly, it sounds like he was just the designated introducer for the GOP on these matters, so points to Frederica Wilson for originality if not for success or content I agree with.

Terri Sewell (D-AL)

She needs a new picture, the one on her Wikipedia page looks like she's forcing her smile. Like I'm one to judge on that, my smiles usually look like someone's off camera with a gun trained on me. She has impressive education credentials- with Oxford under her belt and being a female of color she certainly undermines the Democrats' usual stereotypes about Alabama residents.

She has a very active YouTube account; a lot of her speeches and the like are posted there. But as for TV attention she isn't really making the rounds like Frederica Wilson. Even during the 2017 Alabama Senate Race it looks like she only popped up once on ABC. Her other smattering of appearances mostly seem recent- she's either critical of anyone opposed to the Mueller Investigation or worrying about President Trump's position on Voter ID laws. Safe party-line statements that might as well have come from any other Democrat, unlike Frederica Wilson's very emotionally-driven style which makes for better TV. I can't say it's a more unique approach since Rep. Maxine Waters shares it.

She sponsored 33 pieces of legislation. She had 3 laws, 1 concurrent resolution, 1 resolution, and 7 amendments passed. Two of her laws, plus her resolution and concurrent resolution, related to the civil rights movement: honoring participants and victims, as well as calling for House members who participated to have their stories taken down by the Office of the Historian.

8 bills for the 2017-2018 session, though none have made it passed being introduced. Kind of odd since I'd think her Rural Septic Tank Access act would be a winner

with Republicans given their dominance in such areas, but the bill has barely been in for a month. She sponsored 7 bills introduced in 2015-2016, and of those 2 became law. One renamed a building, the other was a trifle more substantial by awarding a Congressional Gold Medal to civil rights marchers *(not a reflection on her, but given how her party says the GOP is racist I don't see how this bill could possibly have gotten to Obama's desk since the House and Senate were under GOP control- the GOP certainly didn't pass it for optics since no one knows this law exists!)*. 2013-2014 saw another 4 bills from her; 1 became a law. This was another civil rights one *(that the allegedly racist GOP should not have passed)*- it provided a Congressional Gold Medal to victims of the Sixteenth Street Baptist Church bombing. Her first term, 2011-2012, saw her sponsoring one bill but it did not go farther than being introduced.

Rep. Sewell had one concurrent resolution for the 2015-2016 session, which was agreed to both in the House and the Senate. It related to the ceremony for awarding the Congressional Gold Medals, that her law allowed for. She had only 3 resolutions, introduced 2011-2012. One of these passed- directing the Office of the Historian to take down oral histories from House members involved in the Selma to Montgomery civil rights marches and the civil rights movement in general *(you know what I'm thinking- why would the racist GOP let this pass too; why would the sexist GOP even approve stuff from a female minority Congresswoman)*.

She had the same 100% record as her Florida colleague Daniel Webster on 2017-2018 amendments. Two introduced, two approved. For 2015-2016 she had 7 amendments, 5 of which passed.

Martha Roby (R-AL)

I'm just going to finish up with Alabama's 2011 Freshmen. TIME Magazine recently noted that she was facing a difficult election because she said of President Trump, when he was still a candidate, that his decade-old comments on the Hollywood Access tape about what celebrities could get away with *(proven true when the Harvey Weinstein story broke and the later MeToo stories, I'm wondering if framing it as saying Trump was talking solely about himself was an effort to deflect from that particular open secret of what Weinstein and other Democrat donors had been up to)* made him an unacceptable Presidential candidate. Trump eventually endorsed her, and she won the Alabama primary. And that's about it as far as national coverage goes.

She has sponsored 22 pieces of legislation in her 7 year career. Her only true success was one concurrent resolution. Three of her bills passed the House, but that's the best they did. No wonder she gets no coverage, she's in the back of the backbench, though that one concurrent resolution of hers that cut funding to Planned Parenthood should have gotten way more attention than it apparently did *(it apparently received almost NO attention, rather odd given how that's usually a hot-button issue in the mainstream media, at least when a man threatens it)*.

She's done 3 bills for 2017-2018, with two having passed the House. The other went nowhere. She did 6 bills in 2015-2016. 1 passed the House, the other 5 *(including the "Unsecured Server Act of 2016")* went nowhere. For 2013-2014 we see 4 bills sponsored, only one passed the House, but no further action was taken. That particular bill had either a descendant or was recycled for 2017-2018, becoming one of the bills that session to pass the House. Her first term, 2011-2012, saw three bills introduced but none went anywhere.

She proposed a Joint Resolution that went nowhere in 2017-2018- a Constitutional Amendment that would limit government spending per fiscal year, keeping it from exceeding "certain revenue received" during that year. This was recycled from 2015-2016, when it also went nowhere, which was recycled from 2013-2014.

She had one Concurrent Resolution that was agreed to in 2015-2016, which restricted funding to Planned Parenthood among other things.

She has one resolution for 2017-2018, but that didn't gain legs. There was one resolution for 2013-2014 which also went nowhere.

Mo Brooks (R-AL)

Last of the 2011 Freshmen from Alabama. I only picked that year because that's when Frederica Wilson entered; I'm just showing some of her contemporaries in the House.

Mo Brooks is seen quite often in the media, though he does not make a show of himself. For those inclined towards prayer, send one his way since he had surgery for prostate cancer in December 2017.

He sponsored 42 pieces of legislation. None of his bills became law, though one did pass the House recently. Otherwise, his only legislative achievement were 3 Resolutions that were agreed to. Sorry Mo Brooks, pretty much the only reason I don't put you behind Frederica Wilson as a backbencher is that you are Vice-Chairman of a subcommittee and your TV performances are predictably tame, befitting your record.

2017-2018 saw 9 bills from him. One has passed the House. He introduced 8 from 2015-2016 but none got beyond being introduced. 7 bills came from him in the 2013-2014 session but they did not go anywhere. His first session, 2011-2012, saw 4 bills introduced. This completes his record of no bills going anywhere, unless the sole one that passed the House in 2018 picks up steam.

He introduced one Concurrent Resolution in 2017-2018, which went nowhere.

One Joint Resolution came from him in 2013-2014, but it failed to go beyond being introduced.

There were two resolutions from him in the 2015-2016 session, but they were only introduced, no progress was made. One resolution came from him in 2013-2014, which would've allowed the President to be sued over breaking with their Constitutional duties relating to immigration, but it was sent to the Congressional gulag known as a "committee" where it remains, fate unknown, to this day.

He introduced just one amendment in the 2017-2018 session, to defund Amtrak, but it failed. He did better with his 4 amendments 2015-2016. 2 of those passed. Both related to illegal aliens- one impacted whether they could enlist, the other prevented funds for being used to provide them housing assistance. Makes sense- entering the U.S. illegally is a criminal act, and any U.S.-born criminal is subject to a law which states they aren't allowed to profit from their crime. One of his two Amendments in 2013-2014 passed. Incomprehensibly enough for the modern Democrat Party, the amendment that passed stopped money from being used in any non-treaty executive agreement with Russia that would relate to missile defense or giving Russia information on our missile programs. In other words- a Republican introduced something which the Republican House agreed on that limited a Democrat President's ability to be soft on Russia. My how times change. From 2011-2012 he introduced 2 amendments, and these passed.

Eric Crawford (R-AR)

Apparently he was a news anchor.

Though until now I don't think I've ever heard of him, unlike Mo Brooks and Frederica Wilson. He's sponsored 66 pieces of legislation. A bunch of it dealt with the EPA and farmers. Out of that figure, only 9 items- 9 amendments- went into effect. Or would have if the bills they were attached to went anywhere, I really don't know if that happened with any of the bills that any amendment referenced in this volume was attached to, but that's a tertiary measure since I'm only counting if items the person proposed went as far as they could in that area. An Amendment can only go so far- "does it become part of a bill or does it not?".

Crawford sponsored 12 bills so far for 2017-2018. They've only been introduced. 2015-2016 saw a lucky 13 bills. One of them passed the House. One of these bills was for renaming a building, but it went nowhere. Can't even get a darn building renamed… that's low-hanging fruit! His so-called "Sunshine on Government Act", which asked OMB to make a separate website that would link to another website containing reports from the OIG, seems a little haughtily named, more like the "Build A Website So I Can Pretend I Helped With Transparency Act". The website didn't sound particularly useful, and the OIG reports are usually available elsewhere anyway. He was a busy little beaver with his 2013-2014 Bill schedule. 17 introduced, 2 passing the House. Noteworthy for its ambition, one bill called for Constitutional amendments to balance the budget and restrict new entitlement spending. That went nowhere, but the bills that passed the House helped farmers and did something with the SEC that I cannot understand. If I spoke stock market jibber-jabber, I wouldn't need to write this to make money! In his first session, 2011-2012, he sponsored 9 bills. One passed the House before stalling, the rest didn't even get that far.

There were three Joint Resolutions to his name, in the 2013-2014 session. Much like his bill for a Constitutional amendment on entitlement spending that went nowhere, one resolution called for just such a Constitutional amendment and also went nowhere. The other two also made no progress, and were similar resolutions about appropriations.

His 2011-2012 session saw one resolution, which went nowhere.

His solitary Amendment for 2017-2018 was agreed to: an amendment to a Department of Defense appropriations bill, which if I read it right gave extra funding to Explosive Ordinance Disposal equipment upgrades. Might actually save a life, unlike certain other laws such as those renaming a building. 2015-2016 saw 5 amendments- 1 withdrawn, 4 approved. Another useful amendment- he amended a Department of Interior funding bill so that the money appropriated couldn't be used to fund activists or other such groups to influence legislation at the state and national level. Basically, it stopped a government agency from using taxpayer money to make the public want to give said government agency more money and power. 4 amendments came from him 2013-2014, 3 passed and one was withdrawn. Bookending this section, there was just one Amendment for the 2011-2012 session, which dealt with the EPA and was agreed to.

Steve Womack (R-AR)

He's about as old as my parents, but he went gray MUCH earlier. I don't know why, he only sponsored 29 pieces of legislation. Seems low-stress. Only one item ran its full course- a law was made creating a commemorative coin. Yet he's now Chairman of the House Budget Committee.

In the 2017-2018 session, he introduced two bills that went nowhere. Neither dealt with budget matters. There were 9 bills 2015-2016, one passed the House, none really had anything to do with the budget. He had 8 bills 2013-2014, one of which passed the House. One of the bills dealt with taxes and states and businesses, but that went to the House Judiciary Committee so I don't think that counts totally as a budget item, since it looked like it was about getting money rather than spending it. He had 5 bills in his first session, 2011-2012. The first bill he introduced became a law- creating a U.S. Marshals commemorative coin or something. Tommy Lee Jones on the heads side and Daniel Roebuck on the tails side, no doubt. He also had a "Government Shutdown Prevention Act" in March of 2011, which passed the House, and I guess didn't work too long because 2 years later the government did shutdown.

His only Joint Resolution in 2017-2018 went nowhere; it was designed to stop people from desecrating the U.S. flag via Constitutional amendment. Might've gone somewhere if Hillary were President, she once supported such a thing. Aside from bills, all he did 2015-2016 was introduce a Joint Resolution that went nowhere. Pretty much the same resolution as in 2017-2018.

Finally we get to something 2017-2018 that relates directly to the budget: a concurrent resolution that was placed on the calendar. He had another concurrent resolution that session so far, but it went nowhere too. He introduced one Resolution 2017-2018, but nothing came of it. Not budget related.

So… how *did* he end up Chair of the Budget Committee? Maybe there's a different metric?

Paul Gosar (R-AZ)

I thought he quit or something, but I was wrong. They should update his picture at Congress.gov- it looks horrible and doesn't look like his current one. Like a High School picture gone bad or something.

Also, he's sponsored 214 pieces of legislation. Wow. He wins this volume- 5 laws and 76 amendments that were agreed to. With all of this you'd expect him to be on TV as much as Frederica Wilson, or you'd expect Rep. Wilson to have done as much as Gosar to earn that airtime. Nope. Gosar does not put his face on TV very much.

19 bills for 2017-2018, 3 of them passed the House. 2015-2016 saw 35 bills, one became law. Probability dictates that would be the case; generally such action is described as "shotgunning it". Too bad it just renamed a building. This powerhouse churned out 23 bills 2013-2014. 3 of them became law- two renamed a building, the other had something to do with a Native American tribe and the government and water rights. The description was quite verbose; I couldn't figure out what was going on. As for hitting the ground running, his first session from 2011-2012 saw 24 bills, 2 just passed the House, while a third bill passed the House, the Senate, President Obama, and became law- it affected the authority of the Secretary of the Interior in certain matters. Pretty good for someone who just got there.

He had one Joint Resolution for 2017-2018, which didn't go anywhere. Same for his 2015-2016 Joint Resolution.

There were 2 Concurrent Resolutions in 2015-2016, but nothing came of them.

Just like above, there were 2 regular Resolutions from 2015-2016, but nothing came of those. He had 3 for 2013-2014 which also went nowhere. There were also 2 resolutions 2011-2012 that went nowhere.

For 2017-2018 he had 6 amendments and only 2 succeeded. He must've been taking a break, because 2015-2016 saw 54 amendments. 45 were agreed to. He warmed up 2013-2014 with 28 amendments. 21 were agreed to. He started off in his first session, 2011-2012, with 14 amendments. 8 were agreed to.

David Schweikert (R-AZ)

Don't be fooled- he's not on TV much either. He just looks like actor Walter Burke. He's in Rep. Wilson's weight class when it comes to sponsored legislation, 81 pieces of it. Out of that, his only successes were with 6 amendments.

He sponsored 8 bills 2017-2018. One of those bills passed the House, the rest did not make it even that far. For his 21 bills 2015-2016, only one passed the House, but it didn't go beyond that. 11 bills for 2013-2014, with one passing the House again. The Senate must hate this guy or something, since what little that does get through the House stalls in the Senate. Finishing up, we have his first session, 2011-2012, in which he sponsored 14 bills and yet again one of them passed the House only to smash into the brick wall known as the Senate.

From the 2015-2016 session we have one Joint Resolution which went nowhere. His 2013-2014 Joint Resolution to go nowhere involved proposing a Constitutional Amendment that would make sure the budget stayed balanced. Silly goose. It seems he and Rep. Crawford copied each other that session, while Rep. Roby would try a similar stunt 3 years later to no avail, failing to learn from history obviously. Schweikert had two Joint Resolutions from 2011-2012. One called for another Constitutional Amendment. That would make it so that the Federal Government needed approval from a majority of state legislatures before increasing the debt. The other called for term limits, the poor insane fool. Cursed from the beginning, no wonder only a handful of his pieces of legislation passed.

His only Concurrent Resolution to date was in the 2011-2012 session, and called for a commemorative postage stamp for the guy who drew "Family Circus" comics. Can't even get a stamp for the "Family Circus" guy… shouldn't have tried for those term limits. I can imagine how it went- House Speaker Boehner: "Yous to a nice Concurrent Resolution there buddy" House Minority Leader Pelosi: "Be a shame if somethin' happened to it" Boehner: "If yous limit us guys' toims, we can't be 'round to protect small helpless legislation like this…"

2015-2016 saw 4 resolutions which went nowhere. Same with the 2 he introduced in the 2013-2014 session. There were 3 resolutions that went nowhere in the 2011-2012 session, one of them looked like it was aimed at legislative pork because it would've "[prohibited] the consideration of any bill or joint resolution carrying more than one subject." Term limits, an end to pork, stopping America's debt crisis: this man is out of control.

He had 6 amendments 2015-2016: two withdrawn, two failed, two agreed to. One of the failed amendments was an ecologically-friendly one, calling for investigating the idea of reducing department vehicles for the Department of Transportation and investigate ride-sharing options, amended to a bill calling for reducing the funding that the Department of Transportation would receive. Seems like you'd want to cut vehicles to cut costs, but what do I know. His sole amendment for 2013-2014 failed. In the 2011-2012 session he had 5 amendments, and out of that 4 passed. One was withdrawn.

Jeff Denham (R-CA)

Rounding out today's edition, we have Jeff Denham. Yes, I know this was Republican-heavy, but A: I'm just doing it in order by the state and B: the Freshmen for 2011-2012 were largely Republicans. As for Denham, he has been making a few TV appearances this year, but was kind of an unknown on the TV circuit before that. I didn't watch, but from the titles of the links I assume it has something to do with immigration reform and him vs. the rest of California during his re-election bid.

With 82 pieces of legislation, Denham is in the Wilson/Schweikert tier. Both of them had 6 success stories, so what has Denham done? 6 laws, 3 Concurrent Resolutions, and 16 amendments were successful. Though his laws were better than Gosar's, Denham is still runner-up in this volume because he loses on quantity of achievements by a grossly unfair margin.

2017-2018 saw him sponsor 11 bills, with 3 passing the House. 2015-2016 was far more productive: 16 bills sponsored, with 2 becoming law. You have him to thank for the "Federal Property Management Reform Act of 2016" and "Federal Assets Sale and Transfer Act of 2016". Again with the 2 laws, out of the 15 bills in the 2013-2014 session. The "Department of Veterans Affairs Expiring Authorities Act of 2014", and some law modifying requirements relating to enhancing access to pipeline safety documents. A third bill had passed the House. He was off to a running start in his first session, 2011-2012. 14 bills- 2 became law,3 others passed the House. I think his first law, establishing a date for counting the 2012 election votes, was a gimme. The free space on a legislator's bingo card, given out to the popular ones I guess. Or they drew from a

hat. Who knows. His other law was less of a gimme-
"Veteran Skills to Jobs Act".

Mr. Popular's 2015-2016 Concurrent Resolution
"[p]roviding for a conditional adjournment of the House of
Representatives and a conditional recess or adjournment of
the Senate" passed the House and the Senate. Mr. Popular
struck again, or first, in the 2011-2012 session 4
Concurrent Resolutions with 2 being approved by the
House and Senate. Both of the approved resolutions seem
to have the same title, and involved authorizing the use of
Capitol Grounds for a Peace Officer memorial service.
His two resolutions in the 2017-2018 session didn't make
it. Neither did his solitary resolution in the 2011-2012
session.

He had 7 amendments for 2017-2018, all of which
were agreed to. All three of his amendments in the 2015-
2016 session were agreed to. He had 3 amendments in the
2013-2014 session, but only one was agreed to. One failed,
the other was withdrawn. He had 5 amendments in the
2011-2012 session, and all 5 were agreed to.

Go forth to thine midterms, ye of these districts!!!

-J. Patters

Voting is your civic duty. Your vote sends a message to your representatives. Often, they will misinterpret it, but it's not hopeless.

www.ingramcontent.com/pod-product-compliance
Lightning Source LLC
Chambersburg PA
CBHW031359250726
48656CB00016B/2369